The Chapters

The First Nest _____ 4

The First Cat Pounces _____ 6

Growing Up _____ 8

Broken Wings _____ 13

A New Beginning _____ 16

More Storms to Weather _____ 22

Starting Over _____ 25

Who Am I? _____ 26

A New Relationship _____ 29

The Last Straw _____ 36

Stretching My Wings to Shelter Others _____ 42

Flying Solo _____ 46

My Soul Mate _____ 50

Finding Faith _____ 54

Fallen from Flight _____ 59

From Sparrow to Eagle _____ 63

The First Nest

The birds nest beside the streams and sing among the branches of the trees.
Psalm 104:12

I grew up in Brunswick, a suburb of Melbourne, in a three-bedroom house with my mother and father. At first Dad didn't have much to do with me, until I began to say 'Dad'. My mother said that from that point on I could do no wrong in my father's eyes. He and I were very close and spent time playing games, talking, laughing and going out. He would take me everywhere with him and I have strong memories of walking down the street holding hands, feeling so proud to be with him that I might burst. This vision of walking with my father is one of the strongest and happiest memories I have from my childhood.

Dad was a carpenter and did a lot of building at home. We had two sheds in our backyard. One for junk and the other was his workshop, with a loo attached. Back in those days it was common to have the loo outside. I loved to 'help' Dad, sitting up on his workbench. He always smelt of wood, and still to this day I love the smell of freshly sawn wood as it reminds me of him. Dad built three houses over the years but had sold them by the time I was born, and the house we lived in was his childhood home.

One time I smashed up some chalk and mixed it with water to look like a bottle of milk. I gave it to Dad to drink but I got scared it might make him sick, so I told him just

DEDICATION

For my children, who have walked much of this journey with me. Thank you for your encouragement and inspiration. I am extremely proud of each one of you.

Also, to survivors of domestic violence who have travelled a similar road. Our stories connect us. And to those who have not yet found the courage they need. May this book be a small light on your path to freedom.

Acknowledgements

I am gratefully indebted to my friends and family who prompted me to write my story. Without their encouragement I would never have been able to do it. There are too many to name, but their friendship and support have meant the world to me.

My thanks go to Pastor Richard and Pastor Helen Kobakian whose weekly messages helped me become the woman I was meant to be. I am grateful to my church family at LifeHouse Church for always helping me to aim for my best. Pastor Wendy Vella gave me the final push that I needed to write down my memories. Thank you for believing in me Wendy.

And lastly, my thanks go to my editor, Breallyn Wesley, who encouraged me to grow, to be strong and not afraid to tell it like it is. Thank you for arranging my writing into the story I've always wanted to tell.

Picture a little sparrow, pecking up crumbs in a courtyard on a winter's day. Look closely – cats surround her, waiting to pounce. The sparrow is small, meek and vulnerable. She lives under the heavy cloud of threat and danger.

What would it take for this fragile bird to rise up, to out-fly the dangers that surround her, and transform into a strong, proud eagle, who guides and protects others within her range?

The story of this transformation is my life story.

as he was about to drink it. He laughed and chased me up the side of the house, pretending to be angry.

My mother went out a lot on weekends, on mud scrambles on her motorbike. This left a lot of time for Dad and I to be together. I am grateful to have these memories of him, they have always stayed with me, even though he passed away over 60 years ago.

When I was six and a half my Dad died. My whole world changed forever that day. I never got to say goodbye to my Dad, or to attend his funeral. In those days, children weren't encouraged to talk about their feelings during times of loss, so no one ever spoke to me about my father. Even my mother never spoke of him until many years later. To me it was like he was there one day and gone the next. He was everything to me and when he died there was a huge gap that no-one else could ever fill.

I was sent to my Aunt Nancy's place to stay for a month while my mother recovered. My Aunt had four children, three girls and a boy who were close in age to me, only eight years between the five of us. I got on well with my cousins and we had lots of fun together going off on our own to explore the things around us. One day we were walking through the local quarry and suddenly I slipped into a mud hole. It felt like quick-sand and I was really scared, but my cousin Phil, who was a year younger than me, pulled me out. I think we were about nine and ten at the time.

The First Cat Pounces

He has hidden like a bear or a lion, waiting to attack me.
Lamentations 3:10

I slept in the lounge room while I stayed at Aunt Nancy's. One night Aunt Nancy's husband, Uncle Ken, came into the lounge room after everyone had gone to bed. He molested me. I was so frightened I couldn't speak. I felt that what was happening was wrong but I was so shocked I just lay there. What he was asking me to do didn't make sense to me, and I didn't know how to get out of the situation, so I just did what he wanted, even though I didn't want to.

My Aunt must have woken up because she called out to him to come to bed. Then she came into the dark lounge room and asked him what he was doing. He said he was just saying goodnight. They both went to bed. At the time I was too young to understand what had happened, but I felt bad and ashamed and dirty and didn't understand why. I never told anyone about it.

From then on when I stayed at my Aunt's house I always slept in the same room with my cousins. Whenever Uncle Ken came to kiss me goodnight, all those feelings of discomfort, shame and guilt would come flooding back to me even though at that age I didn't understand why or even remember what he had done. I guess my mind couldn't deal with it so I learned to block it out. However, those feelings would never leave me, and I carried them with me until the day he died. I tried to make sure I was never alone with him and I would cringe and turn my face away whenever he came near me. As I look back and reflect on what Uncle Ken had done to me and how it affected my life for many, many years after, as I am writing this down it makes me wonder if it happened more than once and I was able to block it out. I mean , how could one incident have such a strong effect on such a young child. Thank God I don't dwell on it because it is in the past where it belongs.

Growing Up

Where once there were thorns,
cypress trees will grow.
Isaiah 55:13

Life changed after my dad died. I still enjoyed school and remember some good times playing with other children. I had a friend next door and one across the road, and I was allowed to play in their homes, and sometimes go out with them and their parents. There was also a family we knew who had a girl my age, and they would take me to their holiday house down the coast, in Rosebud. They would really spoil me, and treated me like I was their own child. We would go to the beach, the carnivals and circus and they would always buy me something to take home. Through these families of my friends I got a taste of how I thought 'normal' families lived. I felt very lucky during that period of my life.

My mother had a close friend named Vera who we would often visit. I called her Aunty Vera and her husband Uncle Harry. They had an adult son Johnny and an adult daughter Rita who I called Uncle and Aunt, which was traditional back in those days. Everyone was either Aunt, Uncle, Mr. or Mrs. We spent almost every Christmas with them. They always treated me like I imagine a grandchild would be treated. They would spoil me with gifts on my birthday and at Christmas. I even got to be a bridesmaid at Aunt Rita's wedding.

Christmas lunch at Aunt Vera's was extra special. The table was especially nice and dessert was always Christmas pudding. In my youth the tradition was to put money into the pudding for kids to find and I was the only child at the table. Back then the money was in pounds, shillings and pence. Uncle Johnny would play tricks on me, saying "look up there, there's a spider," and while I was looking away he would hide more money under the pudding. He did it every Christmas. I loved it because it made me feel really special and of course the money was nice to have. Uncle Johnny would take me to the shop to spend it during our stay, as we usually stayed there for a night or two. I'm so glad to have these happy Christmas memories.

My mother became very strict after my dad died. I felt I was always in trouble for one thing or another. She became physically and mentally abusive to me, always putting me down by saying I wasn't good enough.

One time I made a skirt at school and got a 10/10 mark for it. I was very proud, but my mother said the stitching was crooked, it was too short and a terrible colour. I felt this was terribly unjust because, in my mother's words, she herself couldn't sew a straight line if you paid her. My Aunt Nancy was a good sewer, and I had developed a close relationship with her. I suspect my mother was jealous of our closeness, and this was why she criticized my skirt so heavily. Aunt Nancy was always kind to me. She would make me cups of tea or help me around the house whenever she came to visit. Many years later she told me she felt like my mother treated me like a slave.

When I was about thirteen my mother accused me of taking her stockings and wearing them. She gave me a belting and almost strangled me. I had scratches on my face and when I went to school I had to tell them the cat had scratched me. Luckily my Aunt Enid, who was staying with us at the time, pulled her off me. I didn't take those stockings, but several weeks later I found them and decided to wear them. After all, I had already been punished, so why not.

I had a very vivid dream life during the years I was growing up.

I had several out of body experiences, lying in bed and feeling like I was on the ceiling looking down at myself sleeping. I often dreamt of flying and of falling, but would wake before I fell. I also dreamt vividly of the house next door. I would walk in the front door and find snakes laying on the floor in circles. I had to walk from the front door to the back door without touching a snake, otherwise they would spring up like a cage and I would be trapped. It was terrifying. I would wake up shaking in a cold sweat if I had been caught by the snakes in my dream.

My mother used to tell me she had 'picked me up out of the gutter when nobody else wanted me,' and called me a 'tramp' if I walked around the house with no shoes on. I used to talk in my sleep and also answer if you asked me a question, so my mother would often ask me if I was 'doing things with boys.' Sometimes I would wake up when my mother questioned me. She seemed obsessed with this question and would threaten to put me in a home if I ever did.

My mother was sick a lot of the time, from when I was about eight years old. She suffered with bad kidneys and a weak heart, and eventually one of her kidneys was removed.

One night, when I was about eleven, my mother was drying clothes over the open fire in the lounge room, when she bent over too far and her dressing gown caught fire. She suffered third-degree burns to her back and buttocks. The doctors didn't expect her to live the night, her burns were so bad. It was six weeks before I could visit her because she was so sick and at risk of infection.

Then, when I was about twelve, my mother had a stroke which left her with limited mobility in her leg. As a result of her illnesses, I did all the cooking, cleaning and shopping from then on.

Whenever my mother was admitted to hospital my Aunt Enid and her son William would come and stay with me. William was twenty-five; thirteen years older than me. Sometimes he would take me with him when he coached a young men's wrestling team, or to the movies. When he travelled interstate for the wrestling team he would take both me and his fiancé with him. My Aunt Enid and cousin William were both kind to me, and I found myself wishing my mother would stay in hospital forever. When I was around other people I would feel good and be able to laugh, enjoy myself and relax. I didn't feel this way when I was with my mother.

My mother had the ability to make everyone else laugh, and other family members would tell me how lucky I was because she was so funny. But things were different when the two of us were alone.

Broken Wings

*Like lions they open their jaws against me,
roaring and tearing into their prey.*
Psalm 22:13

As teenage girls often do, I kept a diary full of my escapades of wagging high school with my friend, and the things we would do. I was always a bit of a loner at school and had only one friend. If she was away from school I would sit on my own during breaks. So, when she suggested wagging school I went along with her so I wouldn't be on my own. I was petrified my mother would find out, but the rebelliousness came out in me anyway.

My friend and I would hang out at the shops and go to Coburg Lake. Sometimes we would meet up with other people she knew, mostly boys. Schools weren't as diligent back then about attendance I guess, because we were never caught out.

One day when I was about fourteen I came home from school to find my cousin William there alone. My mother was in hospital again, so William and Aunty Enid were staying with me. William had taken a day off work. After chatting for a while he pulled out my diary which he had found in my room. He then threatened to show it to my mother if I didn't have sex with him. I was afraid of what my mother would say and do so I gave in to William's demands. My mother often threatened to put me in a home if I misbehaved, and I believed that she would do it. From then on, William continued to abuse me over the next two years, until he got married. Sometimes he would take me to his place to have sex and even expected me to enjoy it. It was horrible. I loathed those times. I would concentrate on the white ceiling in his flat and pretend that I was somewhere else until he had finished. I tried to block out that it had happened at all, so I don't remember many of the details.

The rest of the time William was kind to me in buying me lollies and smokes. This added to my confusion, guilt and shame. I felt like a prostitute in a way, because I would take the things he gave me. This made me feel even worse about myself. It was during this time in my life I often held my hand over a boiling kettle. I deliberately scolded the skin on my hand as I made my mother a cup of tea, just to feel some sense of control over my suffering. I can still remember the smell of William's body odour and, to this day, over fifty years later, that smell makes me feel sick. Even the smell of Weeties and Weetbix, which he ate a lot, turns my stomach. Despite my efforts to block out what he was doing, I could never block out his smell.

Words can never describe how alone I felt during this period of my life. I lived in fear of someone finding out my secret, especially my mother. She would have put me in a girls' home straight away, or at least that's how I felt. I was too ashamed and embarrassed to talk to anyone because I believed they would judge me as a bad person and call me names. Any men I came into contact with made me feel uncomfortable. I always expected they would do or say something, I was always suspicious of their intentions. I felt like a little sparrow in a yard full of cats, unable to fly yet, unable to escape, trying to hide behind bushes in the garden, anywhere out of sight. I was so depressed I tried to kill myself. I tried to strangle myself with some wool. Of course, it kept breaking and just made me feel like I couldn't even do that right.

During this same time, I became sexually active. I rebelled against my mother's poor opinion of me and did exactly what she was already accusing me of doing. It was a bit like my attitude toward the stockings — if you're going to get accused of doing something you might as well do it. By the way, this is not an attitude I would now recommend. I also began to do badly at school and failed Year Ten.

A New Beginning

*For I am like a tree whose roots reach the water,
whose branches are refreshed with the dew.*
Job 29:19

When I was sixteen I left school and got a job in the city as a clerical assistant. This was a new beginning for me where I could meet other people and make new friends. I still had to do everything at home, but I didn't mind except for Sunday. On the weekends I got to sleep in after working all week, but Saturdays were for cleaning and shopping when I got up. That was fine, but on Sunday I had to be up early enough to have the ironing done before nine o'clock in the morning, so my mother could watch *World of Sport* on TV. The only place to plug in the iron was in the lounge room where the TV was. Maybe that's why I've never liked ironing; now that I'm on my own I don't even own one! I buy clothes that don't need ironing.

Not long after I started work I met my first husband, Don. We met at a wedding of all places. I arrived with the groomsman and came home with the best man, literally! We were together every weekend from that day on. I wasn't allowed out during the week because I had to get up for work. Don was seven years older than me and he swept me off my feet. I think I fell in love almost instantly, although I wasn't really sure what love was.

I was very close with my friend from across the road. So she was the one I turned to when I fell pregnant at seventeen. She convinced me to talk to her Mum, who convinced me to tell my mother. When I went to tell my mother I was pregnant, she was in hospital, so she couldn't yell at me or punish me. I took Don with me because he said he wanted to marry me. I think the only thing my mother was concerned about was the fact that I was getting married. In those days it was a disgrace to your family if you were pregnant if you weren't married.

Don and I were married after only four months of being together. It was a very small wedding with just my immediate family and our neighbours. Don's family were all in Newcastle, New South Wales. His mother had put him in a home when he was born and he stayed there until he was sixteen when he moved out and supported himself. His mother had another child whom she raised, but was still unable to bring Don home, which was sad for him. I continued to work after our marriage until I was eight months pregnant. I believed us both to be in love. After all, he was my saviour because I didn't have to go into a home for unmarried mothers. I hadn't had much love in my life to compare my feeling for Don to, and my attitude was that if it felt good and it felt right it must be love. And I was happy, very happy. We would go out to movies, dances, parties, even a country road car racing rally two days before our daughter was born. The night she was born we went dancing as well. I think that is why she was born early. Too much shaking up, I guess.

So, I was finally free of my mother's tyranny, and with someone I loved. Although we did live with my mother until our baby was about one, she was much better toward me. But whenever Don and I had a disagreement she would always take his side. I didn't really care though because I had someone who loved me, so her opinion of me wasn't as important as it had been, although I still found myself seeking her approval in everything I did. Even on my wedding day I asked her permission to drink a beer. Women drank and smoked during their pregnancies back then, unaware of any health risks. My mother was good with my daughter and also supportive of my parenting, which was really surprising considering how she had always put me down beforehand. I hadn't been around babies much so I knew next to nothing of how to look after them. However, for me, becoming a mother was the best thing in the whole world.

When our daughter was about nine months old I got a job in a factory where they had childcare. I loved being a full-time mum but it was time to pull my weight financially. Don and I worked in the same place for a while and that was really good but then Don got a job working for travelling carnivals when our daughter was about one and half. So we bought a caravan and travelled around with them. Don worked on the rides and sometimes I would look after the other children while their parents worked. We were both happy, or so I thought. But then I became pregnant with our second child and it seemed like just out of the blue Don wanted to leave. He took me to my Aunt Nancy's place to stay.

I was in shock, I didn't understand what was happening or why. Don said he didn't love me anymore and that it was over. I hadn't told him what Uncle Ken had done to me when I was a child and never did, so he didn't know how I felt about him. I had our caravan in the back-yard and I made sure the door was locked when I went to bed. When our second daughter was born, Don came back saying how sorry he was and how much he really loved me. I forgave him and welcomed him back into our lives.

My mother died when I was twenty-two. She had been sick for a long time and eventually her heart failed. Her next-door neighbour found her when she hadn't seen her for a few days. Her funeral was the first funeral I had ever been to, and I found it a bit surreal. I guess I was numb, in shock, as we had started to get along and had a reasonably normal relationship by this time. And then she was gone.

I had become convinced that I was adopted, because of the things my mother would say to me, so after her death I asked the solicitor if there was anything in her will to say I was adopted but there was nothing. I also asked my godmother but she said no as well, so I reluctantly put this idea aside.

After my mother's death, Don and I went to New South Wales to live, so Don could be closer to his mother and brother. Our trip to Newcastle to start a new life was like the honeymoon we never had. We took a week to get there, stopping at various places of interest along the way. We had two children at this stage, both girls; a four-year-old and a one-year-old. We stayed in a caravan park when we first arrived in Newcastle, which was across the road from the beach. Sometimes we would walk across the road to the rocks on the beach and pick oysters. We would go home and make oyster sandwiches. The girls loved doing that, especially eating them. We were happy again; our own little family.

We hadn't been in Newcastle for long when I found out I was pregnant again. I had gotten pregnant on our trip up there. We had been arguing quite a bit over money, like many couples do, but Don decided he wanted to leave again, and this time said that he had found someone else. I was devastated. I didn't know what to do. I was in a different state with two children, one on the way and no family of my own nearby. Thankfully a new friend I had made offered to let me put the caravan in her back yard.

The woman Don had left me for was a nurse. She worked at the only hospital near where we lived, and happened to be working the maternity ward at the same time that I gave birth to my son. I had gotten a glimpse of her, so I was prepared when she came into my room. She obviously knew who I was as well because she looked really nervous when she did come in. I just said hello and smiled at her. I think that shocked her even more than if I had made a scene.

After all, why make a scene and just upset everyone all over again. Don's relationship with her didn't last long. The day after my baby boy was born, Don decided he had made a mistake again and wanted to come back. So, we all welcomed him back home once again.

One day when my son was nine months old, I had him outside the caravan in his playpen, which I often did in the warm weather. I walked outside to see him trying to push the playpen up the driveway.

It was time to move! We moved our growing family into a three-bedroom house. Would you believe we had trouble fitting all of our things into the new house? Don't ask me where it all went in the caravan, but it did. We got a dog and a cat, and life was good. I was content and thought we were all happy once again. Luckily, I'm an optimist.

Over the ten years of our marriage, Don left me three times. The first two times he left I was pregnant, and when the baby was born he came back. I let him come back because I believed I still loved him and he still loved me and I didn't want to be alone. My biggest fear back then in life was being on my own with my children. When he was around, Don was a good provider, husband and father. We had lots of fun together with the children going for drives, fishing, going to the beach, visiting friends - just being a normal couple. But after a while I think he just got bored. I know he regrets it now. Although we live in different states we are now friends and visit each other from time to time.

More Storms to Weather

*You throw me into the whirlwind and destroy
me in the storm.*
Job 30:22

When our fourth child was eight months old, Don left us again. Amazingly, he stayed through the pregnancy and birth, but once again he left me for another woman. This time I felt it was more than I could bear, and I went for a walk one night and found myself at a church. I don't know what sort of church it was, but I went in, knelt down, prayed and cried my heart out. The pastor of the church came up to me and, instead of offering sympathy and support, he asked me to leave because he had to lock the door. This felt like a slap in the face. It was just another way of reinforcing my insecurities and feelings of shame, helplessness and worthlessness. Again, I was like that little defenceless sparrow. It seemed like even God had turned

His back and given up on me, and didn't want to know me. From that point on, I turned my back on Him and chose to believe He didn't exist, and I raised my children to have the same beliefs.

After leaving that church I went home and swallowed a whole bottle of Valium, then walked to the beach. Valium is a drug used for anxiety and depression, and it helped deaden the mental pain I was feeling. I was struggling with the knowledge my husband wanted to leave again. I felt my children would be better off without me because whenever Don left I was really depressed. I'm not sure what happened next, except I remember waking up in hospital after sleeping for three days.

I was then put into the psychiatric ward and had to have group counselling sessions. Most of the participants were young people who were children of broken marriages suffering depression and drug and alcohol abuse, because they couldn't deal with their parents' break-up. Divorce wasn't as common back then as it is now, and it was difficult for many young people to deal with. These sessions made me feel worse, because I imagined my children going through the same problems. I was admitted to this ward voluntarily, so I decided to discharge myself.

I went home and I vowed to never let anyone - myself included - get me to that state of hopelessness again! Who would look after my children if I died? They needed me to take care of them. So, I accepted the fact that Don was leaving, and I would deal with it as I had with everything else in the past, and I would take care of my children myself.

Don was going interstate to live with his new girlfriend but was still living in our home until he left. He would often drive off to pick his new girlfriend up and take her out. As if this wasn't hurtful enough, his girlfriend would taunt me by making excuses as to why he needed to come back to our house with her in the car. It was usually to pick up a lighter or matches. I knew she was there and one night I just got fed up with her blatant disrespect for me and my children and went out to the car, while Don was inside in the toilet. I dragged her out of the car and threw her over the fence. I yelled and screamed all sorts of abuse at her and threatened that if she ever came back she would get much worse. Don never brought her back to the house again after that. I don't know where I found the strength to stand up for myself, but it did give me some sense of power back over the horrible situation my children and I were in. I was proud of myself, because they had both used me and taken advantage of my good nature.

Don left one night, creeping out in the middle of the night while we all slept. Several months later, Don and his girlfriend split up. His now-ex-girlfriend came to the house and asked me to take him back. She said he missed us all terribly and would sit and look at photos of us and cry. I said I would definitely not take him back, and started divorce proceedings. I threw my wedding and engagement rings into the river.

Starting Over

*Turn to me and have mercy, for I am alone
and in deep distress.*
Psalm 16:5

It was hard being on our own. I remember one time I was unable to pay the electricity bill. In those days, the electricity company would just cut the power off. We had no power, no lights and no hot water for ten days. We had an old kerosene stove for heating and I took the top off it and would boil water to bathe the kids in a bucket. I even cooked on it. We had a portable record player so we would dance and sing to that. At night we would play murder-in-the-dark or hide-and-seek. So, I was able to turn it into a fun time for us all as much as possible. Despite it being difficult, I managed to keep my promise to myself that I would take care of my kids.

Who Am I?

When I was a child, I spoke and thought and reasoned as a child.
But when I grew up, I put away childish things.
1 Corinthians 13:11

After about a year of being on our own, my cousin, the youngest daughter of my Aunt Nancy and Uncle Ken, came to stay because she needed to get away and rethink her life. We spent a lot of time talking about how she was feeling and why. After she went home she wrote me a letter saying she felt I was more like a sister than a cousin. I wrote back and jokingly signed it 'your adopted sister'.

Imagine my surprise when, soon after that, I received a letter from my Aunt Nancy explaining that she was my real mother, and how and why she gave me up for adoption to her aunt. I was twenty-six years old by this time.

So the woman I grew up thinking was my mother was actually my great-aunt, and my Aunt Nancy was actually my biological mother.

Discovering I was adopted made me understand my mother a bit better. The cruel things she said to me made more sense now. My parents' real ages came to light also. When I was born my mother was thirty-nine, not twenty-nine as she led me to believe and my father was fifty-nine. I realised my feeling of being adopted all those years ago had been right all along. The last thing my mother had ever wanted for me was to have a baby out of wedlock —it almost happened, had Don not wanted to marry me. I believe my mother did love me, she just didn't know how to show it, and tried to buy my love with materialistic things. I always had lots of clothes, and a new cassette recorder as soon as they came on the market.

My biological mum was only nineteen when I was born and had had nowhere to go. In those days, there wasn't the governmental financial assistance that single mothers can now receive.

Nancy and I didn't speak about my biological father at this time. I had four children of my own and was too busy to think about it. It is only in more recent years that we have talked of him, and I've found out his name was John. He was Italian, a musician, and he didn't want anything to do with Nancy when he found out she was pregnant.

Finding out that Nancy was my real mother made me happy in a way, because we had grown close when I had been living at her place. Nancy had gotten me a job at the factory where she worked so we spent a lot of time together walking to and from work. We never really developed that close mother-daughter bond that families have, I suppose because that bond needs to be there from the start, however it meant I wasn't alone anymore, that I had a family.

Nancy's husband, Uncle Ken, died from Alzheimer's disease when I was 55 years old. I attended his funeral but only to support Nancy.

Sometime later I told her how Ken had molested me. We had a good discussion about it which made us both feel better, although Nancy stills feels guilty for what her husband did all those years ago when I was six and-a-half years old, and she feels guilty for giving me up when I was born. I don't blame her at all for Ken's actions, and I don't blame her for giving me up to her aunt to raise. I only feel love and respect for her, as she has had a very hard life as well.

Nancy and I now live a couple of hours drive from each other and, as neither of us are in very good health, we don't get to see each other as much as we would like, but we do speak on the phone.

Occasionally we visit each other and stay the night.

A New Relationship

Does a bird ever get caught in a trap that has no bait?
Amos 3:5

After a couple of years without Don, I met a man named Richard at the fruit shop where I worked part-time. He came by often and was very friendly, and always had something funny to say. After a while he came to our house to visit, and meet my children. In some ways he was like a big kid himself, and he got on well with mine. He was also eight years younger than me.

Richard had been raised by his grandparents, and they were very strict with him. When he introduced me to them they didn't like me at first. They believed I was a 'gold digger' and was just after his money (even though I was working.) Eventually, they came to realise they had been wrong about me, and I was able to get on well with his grandparents and the rest of his family. I came to realise that they didn't think Richard capable of much, and did not have a lot of respect for him. I got on particularly well with one of Richard's aunts who had four children of similar ages to my children. We had a lot in common, and I spent a lot of time with her.

After being with Richard for about eighteen months, things began to change. Richard drank too much and began to hit me. The first time it happened I hit him back and he stopped. I was totally shocked. I'd been sexually and mentally abused by men before, but never physically.

He apologised and swore it would never happen again. But it did, and I soon learned it was worse if I hit back. He always apologised later, explaining it had happened because he felt insecure and he really loved me and he was really sorry. He began to pressure me to get married and have a baby, but I kept putting both things off. So, he blamed me for his insecurities and violence. He convinced me that things would change once we got married. He wore me down, and two and a half years after we met we got married.

It was a beautiful wedding. We were married in the park, in front of a fountain. My biological mother and my siblings came for the wedding. My brother gave me away, my sister was my bridesmaid, and my four children were flower girls and page boys. All of Richard's family were there as well, except for his great-grandmother who was too ill. She was in her nineties and housebound, so after the wedding we went to see her in our wedding clothes. It was very emotional and we all had tears in our eyes. She was so grateful we had taken the time to show her how we looked, and it made her feel a part of our ceremony. She was a beautiful person.

On the way to the reception in my sister-in-law's MG convertible, we sat on the top of the back seat and drove through the local bottle shop. Someone took a photo and sent it in to the local newspaper and an article was published saying what we had done. It was such a beautiful wedding, and we had a few days for a honeymoon. It was a wonderful time of our life.

But then once we were married Richard began hitting me again.

He said to me 'You had four kids to another man, but I'm not good enough to have kids with.' This was the reason he gave to continue to hit me. I kept putting off becoming pregnant, but once again I became worn down and got suckered in. I've since learned that men who are physically abusive prey on women like I was; weak and insecure. At that time in my life I would do anything to make others happy and keep the peace. I was still playing the part of that defenceless little sparrow trapped in a yard full of cats, still unable to fly, but at least still alive.

Richard continually reinforced my feelings of worthlessness and convinced me that the abuse was all my fault. Despite the fact that he only had a part-time job to support us all, he convinced me that I wouldn't be able to survive emotionally or financially without him, and that I wouldn't be able to take care of the kids on my own.

If I ever had $4.00 in my purse for milk and bread, Richard would take it saying he would borrow money at the pub. Very rarely would he come back with money after the pub closed at ten o'clock. There were a couple of times when I was so desperate I went to the supermarket, taking my jumper along in a plastic bag. I would put a loaf of bread and a tin of spaghetti on top of my jumper and just pay for those. But under the jumper I would hide more expensive items that we needed but I couldn't afford to buy. It was being so desperate that drove me to do this, and thank God I didn't get caught, because I would have been so embarrassed and ashamed.

A few months after we got married Richard lost his job and never got another full-time job in the six years we were together. Once my youngest son started school I worked part-time as a cleaner. We did have some fun times together with the children. I have fond memories of driving down to Melbourne to visit my family. We would set off at night and make the back seat up like a bed, and the kids would sleep through a lot of the trip. I loved those moments.

Richard would pull over when he was tired and have a sleep. He was a party type person, and he didn't mind when the kids had friends sleep over. One time, I think it was my daughter's birthday, we had a slumber party and our lounge room was just full of kids, blankets and sleeping bags. Most weekends there would be at least one of my children's friends sleeping over for the night. I have always lived by the rule that there is always room in my house for one more. Richard behaved like a normal, happy person on those occasions. He always liked to invite people over for drinks, and at these times he was the life of the party. Everybody loved him. I've since learnt that this can be a common characteristic of abusive men. They can show a very different face to the world from what happens behind closed doors.

Richard was also abusive to my children, mainly my boys. He would drag them around the house by their hair or their ears if they forgot to wash their hands before dinner. Or he would drag them out of bed by their hair or ears if he got home from the pub and saw a toy laying around or rubbish up in the backyard. He verbally and mentally abused my daughters.

I remember one night Richard threatening me as he was standing in the hallway. I picked a wooden elephant up off the buffet and threw it at him. He doubled over in pain, moaning and groaning but I ignored him and ran outside. A short time later he came out promising it was OK and that he was sorry. I didn't believe him. I was hiding under the house and wouldn't even come out when he called the neighbours. I slept under the house all night rather than face him.

My daughter snuck out with a sandwich and cup of coffee for me. He only had one tiny mark on his chest from the elephant, and I had many marks from his hands, yet I was terrified. I still have that elephant thirty-seven years later. It's a reminder of a time I stood up to him. I look at that elephant and smile to myself. It no longer has the tusks because they came off that night, one became embedded in his chest.

There were times in our marriage when we were happy, and our family would laugh together and have fun, but I was always on edge because anything, or even nothing at all, could change Richard's mood and BOOM; he would explode.

I fell pregnant two years into our marriage. One night, when I was eight months pregnant, Richard came home from the pub and, after going in the bedroom to go to bed, he came back out in his underwear and attacked me with the buckle end of a belt. He threatened to belt my daughter as well. He said he would be back to deal with her because she was lying and sticking up for me, so I yelled at her to run. She ran out the back door and I ran out the front door. He had accused me of having someone in the home, even though my daughter and I had just been watching TV.

We both ran next door, and my neighbour went into my home and punched Richard, threatening him not to touch the kids. He then took me to their place for the night. The next day I booked a train for me and the kids to go back to Melbourne to live. At the last minute, Richard talked me into letting him come with us, saying it would be different being around my family and that he would stop drinking.

When we arrived in Melbourne we stayed with my brother. My baby was born, my third son. When he was about six weeks old we found our own place to live. Things were good for a while but then the abuse started all over again. This time Richard said it was because he felt all alone without his family. Abusive men always find an excuse. They say it is never their fault, it's always someone else's.

They hone in on the weak and vulnerable, and at this time in my life, I was weak and vulnerable.

Again I tried to leave, and moved into another house, but somehow Richard found us. I was too scared to tell him to leave, and too scared to let him stay. Then I found out I was pregnant again.

Once again life became good for a while.

I loved being pregnant, knowing a precious child was growing inside me. I mostly had very easy births. My first labour was two and a half hours, and my second baby was born in the ambulance on the side of the road in peak-hour traffic. Ten years later, on the other side of the city when I was on the way to hospital in the ambulance with my fifth baby, I mentioned the birth of my daughter in the ambulance and the paramedic said he had heard about me. I was often mentioned by both the attending paramedics, as it was the first delivery they had assisted in, so the story was well-known. Each birth got quicker until I only just made it to the hospital in time. I had half-hour to spare with my third baby, and only fifteen minutes with my fourth. But six-and-a half years later things changed, and I was in labour for ten hours with my last child. This little girl really took her time. While I was waiting for contractions to become close enough to go to the hospital, I decided to fix our washing machine. I knew my eldest daughter would have to do all the work while I was in hospital, so I wanted to make things easier for her.

My baby girl was very tiny and the doctor wanted her to stay in hospital. I told the doctor I had never gone home without a baby and I didn't intend to start. I convinced him to let me take her home on the condition that I wake her every three hours for a feed.

The Last Straw

God gives justice to the oppressed and food to the hungry.
The Lord frees the prisoners.
Psalm 146:7

The night I came home from the hospital I went to feed my daughter at about 11pm, but Richard wanted me to come to bed. I told him she had to be fed but he argued that she wasn't crying. So I went to bed just to appease him. Within minutes my baby started crying. Richard then accused me of being a bad mother, telling me to get up and feed her. Again and again he would tell me to come to bed, then to get up and feed her. This went on for some time and eventually he became violent. He started punching me and wouldn't stop. He started to choke me and eventually I pretended to faint. He stopped punching me and went to get some water to throw over me to wake me. Then he started punching me again. Eventually he stopped and we went to sleep.

In the morning my face was covered in bruises and I could barely open my eyes. He had broken my nose and my jaw, and damaged the cartilage next to my ear. It still gives me lock jaw at times. I had bruises on my throat for over a month from him choking me and both my eyes were like tiny slits they were so swollen. He immediately vowed never to drink again. But then he said there were two beers in the fridge and did I mind if he finished them? I said 'no, go ahead.' But that was it for me. A turning point. I knew he wouldn't stop at those two beers, and I also knew I had to get away or next time I would be dead. What would happen to my children if I died?

After this severe beating, Richard wouldn't let me out of the house, not even to hang washing on the line. He didn't go to the pub that weekend. My next-door neighbour came over to see me and the new baby, but Richard said I was asleep and wouldn't let her in.

The pattern in our lives had become that, if the children were home when he attacked me, and quite often they were because he was at the pub all day, my eldest daughter would take the others into her room and close the door. The abuse never stopped. Once he even threw his own son out the front door onto the grass. Our son was only eighteen months old at the time. Whenever Richard finished beating me I would pretend everything was fine to try to protect my children and make them feel safe. But it was no way for them to live. And no way for me to live either.

I was finally sure that, although I didn't know what to do or how we would escape, I knew that I had to do it somehow.

Living with abuse of any kind makes you feel useless and unworthy, like you don't deserve any better. But you do. We all deserve happiness, trust, security and most of all love. Abusers like to make you feel useless so you won't leave them. If you are living in a similar situation and experiencing abuse, whether it's mental, physical or sexual, please find the courage to get out. If you don't, it can destroy not only you but your whole family. Children often copy their parents' behaviour, sometimes without even realising it, so these patterns of abusive behaviours have a habit of continuing in each generation. Deep down inside of you there is a place of courage.

Please take that courage and make a better life for yourself and your children. It's not easy, but living in abusive situations isn't easy either.

I used to think I couldn't survive without a man in my life. I believed that I needed the financial and emotional support a man would give me. But I came to realize it wasn't much financial support when my partner didn't give me enough money to feed and clothe me and the kids properly anyway. When we take the step of courage and faith, and leave an abusive situation, we get to take control of our own finances, and the raising of our children, without the fear of being beaten or killed. Many women leave it too late, and die at the hands of the man who should protect them. Make sure that does not happen to you. Help is out there, you just need to find the courage to find it. And if you fail the first time – keep trying, again and again if need be until you succeed.

When Monday came around, Richard had to go to work. He threatened me not to leave the house while he was gone. As soon as he left, my neighbour came over. She had known that something was wrong when he wouldn't let her in the day before. She was very upset by what he had done to me, and said I needed to leave him. I agreed - but where could I go that he wouldn't find me?

After all, I had tried to leave before, but he found me. My neighbour told me about women's refuges. I had never heard of them. So, she took me to her house, as I didn't have a phone at mine, and rang a refuge on my behalf. They said they would call my neighbour when there was a vacancy. A vacancy was a bit harder to find because there were so many of us. I was told to pack our bags to be ready to leave at any time. Richard only worked four hours a day, so I had to go home before he arrived and pretend everything was normal. I confided in my eldest daughter, who was fifteen, about the refuge. She helped me pack our bags, and we hid them under the kids' beds.

Going home, packing, pretending everything was fine and waiting for that phone call was extremely stressful. I expected Richard to find our bags, or that one of the children would see them and say something in front of him. I lived in fear, trying to pretend that everything was normal when all I wanted to do was scream, to get out and run. It was hard to believe we would ever escape. It took the refuge three days to find a place for us, and they were the longest three days of my life. I was on edge the entire time, trying not to upset Richard in any way, and making sure the kids were on their best behaviour. During this time Richard was remorseful for the severe beating he had given me. He told me things like, 'I'm so sorry, I'll never do it again, I love you, I can't live without you, it's because my father used to beat my mother, I'll get help this time I promise, if you leave me I'll kill myself.' It was the usual stage of remorse he went through after he had beaten me, another of the patterns we lived in.

When the refuge centre finally rang, my neighbour came over, right after Richard had gone to work, and said we had to hurry and leave. The kids were at school so I sent my daughter to get them. I rang the school and told them under no circumstances were they to speak to Richard. The refuge had booked two taxis to come and get us. It was getting very close to the time Richard was due home from work, and we were really freaking out.

Eventually one taxi came, and I sent my eldest daughter with some of the kids, while I waited for the second taxi. It felt like an eternity. I didn't even know where we were going; I only knew that a taxi, carrying half my children in it, was going to who-knew-where. I was too nervous to even ask. All I could focus on was getting away before Richard arrived. Eventually the second taxi came. I said goodbye to my neighbour, thanked her for her help and drove away. As we turned the corner of my street, I saw Richard walking up the street with beer cans under his arm. We had only just gotten away in time. My heart still pounds at how close we came to not getting away that day.

I went back to my home one more time, with a police escort, to collect some furniture and belongings. Richard was there, begging my forgiveness again, but having the police there helped my resolve to stand up to him. I thanked my neighbour again, and said goodbye, and

I never went back. It took over a month for the visible scars on my face to disappear, especially the bruises around my throat, but it took over fifteen years before the nightmares stopped. Even now, over thirty years later, I cannot stand anything, even a t-shirt touching my throat, because it makes me feel like I am choking.

The refuge was only a three-bedroom house, and the seven of us shared a room. It was a bit squashy - but we were together, and we were safe. Richard did manage to find us after a few months. One of the workers answered the door and denied we were there. He refused to leave so the refuge called the police and they sent Richard home.

But this meant we had to leave the refuge because it was a breach of security. We then got a house of our own, on the other side of the city. We had been at the refuge for about four months by then.

Stretching My Wings to Shelter Others

We escaped like a bird from a hunter's trap.
The trap is broken and we are free!
Psalm 124:7

Eventually I got a job with the refuge and began helping other women who had come from the same domestic violence we had. Some had suffered a lot worse and a lot longer than we had. I had only been with Richard for seven years altogether; some women endure this type of abuse all their lives. At the refuge we ran counselling and budgeting sessions for the women, as well as self-esteem courses. We assisted with housing and medical issues, schooling for children and appointments with solicitors to discuss legal needs.

We once did a phone-in to research more about women suffering domestic violence and discovered it's not class related. It happens across all walks of life; police officers, doctors and lawyers are as likely to offend as the unemployed; no social class is immune. The more income a man makes, the more likely a woman is to stay with them for the financial support, convinced they won't survive financially without their partner. Women in wealthier situations worry that their children will have to go to public schools, and not have the finer things in life. These women, like those from less wealthy backgrounds, come to terms with the reality that if a parent accepts violence, their children are more likely to accept it as well. None of us want to see our children being abused, or becoming an abuser.

At the refuge, we would sometimes see a woman go back to her partner for a while, before leaving again, like I did with Richard. Each time you leave it becomes easier, and you become stronger. You don't have to give up. On one of these occasions a woman contacted us asking to come back to our refuge. There was no room for her at that time, so I brought her and her two children home to my place.

Another time, a woman with five kids stayed with us for six weeks. I was unable to say no to these women, because I knew the courage it took to make that phone call for help and knew if they didn't get it then they might change their mind and stay with their partner until the next time they were abused, when it might be too late. The woman I welcomed into my home ended up becoming my best friend. Her five children, all similar ages to my four eldest, got on well with mine, and they all adored my little ones. Through my work at the refuge I met my best friends, lifelong friends. One of my good friends has passed away now, but the other, Mary, rings me about once a month and each time we talk it's like we spoke only yesterday. I'm not good at ringing people, it's one of my faults, but she knows how I feel and understands and loves me anyway as any good friend should. Mary lives three hours away from me, but whenever I'm up that way, at my daughter's house, I try to go and visit her.

Sometimes at the refuge, women would arrive with just the clothes on their back. Several times we would later go back to their homes to collect their belongings, and sometimes this would involve altercations with the partner they had left. The police would only attend if they felt it necessary. Most times the police didn't believe the partner would cause any more problems, but sometimes these men would get really angry, and quite often that anger would be directed at us workers. They blamed us for everything, furious that we were forcing them to stay away from their wives and children. The police are a bit more understanding of these issues these days.

One time we went to a woman's house to collect her furniture, but the police didn't think they needed to come. Her partner was there, and luckily for us he was very helpful getting the furniture into the truck we had hired. However, something was telling me not to trust this man. He was being too nice to us, but harassing his partner. So, while he was inside, I popped his bonnet and took out his rotor button which meant his car wouldn't go. When we left he jumped into his car to follow us but his car wouldn't start. I had put the rotor button in his letter box for him to find later.

Working with these women reminded me of how lucky I was to have gotten away. Many women don't survive. One woman dies every week at the hands of their partner. One in four women suffer emotional abuse from the age of fifteen. If you are suffering abuse at the hands of your partner, you are far from alone. We all have a right to have our say without feeling threatened. All partnerships have disagreements, but it doesn't need to end in violence. We should be able to talk over our problems as reasonable adults, not live in fear of saying or doing the wrong thing and being physically and verbally attacked.

Often people say that they would leave immediately if their partner ever hit them - but no one ever really knows what they would do in a situation, until it actually happens. Abused partners have often grown up with violent parents, or feel insecure for other reasons. If you are suffering abuse it's important to remember that it's not your fault, there is nothing to be ashamed of, and there is help out there.

And, of course, this applies to men who are abused by their wives or partners too. It's sometimes even harder for men to access help because there isn't as much support or awareness. It isn't as common for men to be abused but it does happen, and men need to know that they are entitled to help, belief and support as well.

Flying Solo

*Even the sparrow finds a home, and the
swallow builds her nest and raises her young
at a place near your alter, O Lord*
Psalm 84:3

I spent the next eight years on my own, working and trying to raise my children as best I could. It was hard, especially trying to raise teenagers alone. Unfortunately, I made many mistakes, but there were plenty of good times as well. Best of all, we no longer lived with the threat of violence. So life was peaceful. My eldest daughter, who was fifteen at the time I left Richard, was a great help and support to me in looking after the other children, cooking and cleaning, while I worked hard to give us a better life.

In the seventeen years since I had first left home, I had moved home seventeen times. It was mostly due to circumstances, very rarely by choice. But now, during this time of peace, we moved into a home in Brunswick, just up the road from where I had grown up, and I stayed there for the next thirty-seven years. I have more recently moved into a smaller place on my own, but this home in Brunswick, that I moved into when my youngest child was just one year old, was our real family home.

Eventually, my eldest daughter moved into her own place. Then my family began to grow as my first grandchild was born in 1984. Being a grandparent is even more exciting than being a mother.

Watching my child give birth to her own child was absolutely amazing. Knowing that you are responsible for all these people being on this earth is awesome. It has never mattered how many children, grand-children or great-grandchildren I have, they are all just as special as each other, because they are all unique in their own special way. It wasn't easy trying to raise six children, especially when they grew to teenagers, but somehow we got through it. It was not without its dramas, but we had plenty of love to keep us going. Do I have regrets? Absolutely. I made many mistakes as a daughter, a wife, a mother. I can't change the mistakes I've made, I can only learn from them. My mistakes don't define me anymore. I prefer to call them learning experiences. I don't let them define who I am any more. I have tried to encourage other women to find that inner strength to do what they need to do to take control of their lives. Sometimes all they want is a sympathetic ear. One that doesn't condemn or judge whatever their decision is. Just knowing that they are not alone can be all the encouragement they need.

Over the next five years I had five grandchildren, and was kept busy baby-sitting. Sometimes my kids lived with me with their babies for periods of time too. It was a busy and fulfilling time for me. And then of course there was the house moving - I lost count of how many times I helped my two eldest children move, but I became an expert, it was so many times.

In 1990 I found myself unemployed, as I had left the refuge for a break, so I decided to go back to school to get my VCE and then go to university to do a Welfare Studies course which would take another two years. I worked part-time at a health food bakery at night for six months, then I worked at a youth hostel for the other six months during my breaks and day off. I did my VHS through RMIT as a mature age student, and my class were all women. It was a fantastic experience and I did very well in all my subjects, although a couple of times I was caught napping by my English teacher. She would just tell my friends to let me sleep because she knew I had a big family to deal with, and I worked nights as well. Whenever we had assignments coming up for the school holidays I would always ask for them early. When my teachers queried this, saying other students want to wait as long as possible to get their assignments, I told them I preferred to do them while my kids were at school so I could concentrate better in a quiet house. They thought I was unusual, but it made perfect sense to me.

After I finished, I applied to Phillip Institute but they didn't accept me. The person I spoke to said I would find the workload too much with a big family. I explained I had already done my VCE full time and worked part-time, so this would be easy by comparison because it would only be part-time. However, he didn't agree so I went to Melbourne University instead to do a BA. This added an extra two years to my studying, so after three months I decided it wasn't financially viable for me to continue and dropped out. A few years later I did a

Social and Community Services course but realised by the time I finished that, then did two years of Welfare Studies I would be over fifty and find it hard to get a job in the Welfare System. I made the decision to take other employment instead, and ended up cleaning for a living for the next sixteen years. I cleaned houses, then factories and offices. One place I cleaned was Foxtel when it first came to Australia. There were six people working there in the beginning and I cleaned three times a week for half an hour at a time. When I left there, four years later, I was cleaning there twelve days a fortnight, six hours a day and there were five hundred people.

My Soul Mate

*I create the light and make the darkness.
I send good times and bad times.*
Isaiah 45:7

I met my third husband, Steve, at the local footy club where my youngest son played football. Steve was best friends with my son's friend's father. We used to all sit together, watching the footy hanging out, talking and laughing, having fun afterwards. Eventually Steve got up the courage to ask me out. I accepted and we grew closer.

As my feelings for Steve grew stronger and I began to fall inlove with him, I began to have really bad anxiety attacks. I didn't understand why, and my friend suggested I go see her psychiatrist, which I did. And, without even knowing why at first, I began to talk for the first time in thirty-four years about the sexual abuse and rape I suffered as a child and young teenager. I was forty years-old by this time. I can't begin to express the relief I felt at being able to talk through all the pain I had suffered. Even though I had to relive it which brought back memories I had completely suppressed, it was a relief to get it out in the open. The reason for my anxiety was because Steve was like no other man before him. He was a kind, honest and decent man, and I felt unworthy of him because of the shame and guilt I felt over what had happened to me when I was young.

Over several months my psychiatrist helped me to understand that I was only a child and not responsible. The men responsible were adults who took advantage of my innocence and youth. I also suffered self-doubt. My adopted mother's attitude toward me left me insecure and confused, feeling like I had no-one to turn to. All these things left me feeling worthless, useless, a waste of space. I had also suppressed some of the details of the sexual abuse and my psychiatrist helped me understand what had happened, and that I had suppressed those memories as a way of protecting my mind. I was a survivor. I didn't want to be a victim any longer. I wanted to take back my power. It was a time of healing and restoration, a time when this little sparrow was finally spreading her wings.

After my appointments with the psychiatrist, Steve and I would meet up for a coffee, and I told him everything that had happened to me. Steve encouraged and praised me, and reinforced what the psychiatrist said. Eventually I felt much better about myself, worthy of this man who treated me with such respect and love. I felt we were worthy of each other. Steve also taught me not to be afraid to show my feelings and affection. We would often walk down the street holding hands, proud of each other, proud to be in each other's company. I also started to show affection in front of my children, something I'd never done before. I believe seeing our open displays of affection benefited my younger children.

After nine years of being together, we eventually married. It was a beautiful wedding with my children and grandchildren all involved in our special day. All my children were happy for me and accepted Steve into our family.

One of our favourite things to do was go camping in the country. We would often pitch a tent where the only water was a river, and the toilet was a forty-foot drop. We spent many, many wonderful times there as a family, and as time went on my children and grandchildren would take their own children. At least once a year Steve and I would go away on our own, and pitch a tent wherever we felt like stopping. Just a week of driving, pitching a tent and doing whatever took our fancy, with no children arguing and fighting in the background. We were able to just concentrate on each other. These are some of my best memories.

We had many happy times sitting around the campfire at night, talking and laughing. Steve bought a boat, and we would camp right on Major Creek at Mitchelltown, near Nagambie in country Victoria. We spent many hours fishing and swimming there. The first time we went in the boat it was just Steve, my youngest teenage son and me.

We went up the river, and on the way back we got stuck on a tree stump which was just under the water out of sight. We were stuck there for five minutes rocking the boat back and forth before it eventually came off. It felt much longer though. I just sat on the floor of the boat holding on to the seat and laughing because we must have looked so funny to anyone who might have been watching. I was also holding on because I can't swim and I thought that was quite funny as well.

We would take motor-bikes as the children and grandchildren grew older, and they spent many hours riding their bikes. Another time we went camping Steve was on crutches as he had broken his ankle in two places by falling off a loading bay at work. Just before we got to where we camped, on the Mitchelltown road, I felt a bump and looked in the side mirror, to see a wheel coming off the trailer rolling down the road. It looked so funny I started laughing and pulled over. It was pouring with rain, but some really nice people stopped and helped us. Camping was always like that - one adventure after another. We even took our cat with us, and she had a ball chasing animals and insects, jumping around like a kangaroo.

Finding Faith

But those who trust in the Lord will find new strength. They will soar high on wings like eagles. They will run and not grow weary. They will walk and not faint.
Isaiah 40:31

In 2001 my whole perspective on life changed. My youngest son came home one day, talking about God. He said he had found Jesus and that he wanted us to come to church and experience what he had experienced. He said going to church had changed his life, because it wasn't just about going to church, it was about having a relationship with God. He wanted me to see for myself so my life could be changed like his life had.

Of course, I said no. After all, where was God when I needed him all those years ago, when the priest told me to leave the church so he could lock the doors? Why would I want to go to church after that? I had raised all of my children to believe in themselves, not in someone you couldn't even see or speak to. All my life I had relied on myself to get me through the tough times. Even my husband Steve used to accuse me of being too independent, and said I needed to learn to rely on him more. But that was how I had become; if things went wrong I only had myself to blame and that's the way I preferred it.

Eventually, after weeks of nagging from my son, I gave in and went to church. For the first few weeks I was just thinking about how I could get out of going without offending my son. But I did enjoy the music, it was more upbeat than I expected. People would jump and clap with joy to the songs. After a while I started listening to the words of the songs, and then the messages. I started to connect, and relate to what was being said. My belief in only myself started to change. I realised there truly was a God and that He believed in me.

That He had always been there I just hadn't been prepared to acknowledge His existence. He had been walking behind to catch me when I stumbled. I also believe He helped me block out some of the bad things that happened until I was emotionally able to cope with them. After about a year, I made the decision to give myself to God and became a Christian. I was baptised in water and it truly felt like I was reborn, like a new person.

For a long time I had been a very angry person who swore, and yelled a lot at my children. Being in God's presence helped to calm me down and gave me more patience. It gave me an inner peace I had never ever felt in my whole life. I believe God changed my heart from being sad and angry at the world and at life's battles, to feeling content with the good and positive things life has to offer. More open to showing my affections. I did some courses to help me understand what having God in my life meant for me. I understood that Jesus Christ had died on the cross and rose again for all of mankind for ever more, and we were forgiven of our sins, past, present and future if we truly believed that. I realized I wasn't alone any more, that God was here for me, that He had actually always been there for me. I realised that even though I had given up on God He had never given up on me. In those tough times when I didn't know how I was going to feed my children, sometimes a cheque would come in the mail, or someone would give me money they owed me. Something always happened to get us through. And yes, I suffered a lot of hardship, but I got through it. God gave me the ability to switch my mind off and block out the things He didn't think I could handle.

Finally, I had a Father I could trust unconditionally who would never leave me. I remember in those early days of my faith, listening to the song *Hiding Place* by Steve Curtis Chapman. It's a song about Jesus being our hiding place. This song still touches me fourteen years later, because Jesus is my hiding place. He can also be yours if you want Him to be. When the problems life throws at me become too hard to bear, I ask God to take the weight off my shoulders to make it easier for me to deal with. I talk to Him and ask His advice and then listen. It really does work. I know because I have tried coping alone, and I've tried using God's help, and it's much less stressful when you don't have to do it alone. Jesus is always there to help us through.

There is a poem that I really love called ***Footprints in the Sand*** which tells the story of a man walking along a beach talking to Jesus. The man turned around and saw only one set of footprints behind them. He asked Jesus 'why did you forsake me when life was so much harder?' Jesus turned to him and told him 'I would never forsake you son, when you saw only one set of footprints, that was when I carried you.' I just love that thought.

One weekend I went to a seminar. The best way for me to describe it is it was like a cleansing of my heart and soul. One of the many issues we discussed was forgiveness. One of the hardest things for me as a Christian was to forgive those who had hurt me. If you can't find forgiveness in your heart then you dwell on what has happened and it makes it hard to move forward, and those who have hurt you win. If you can put the hurt behind you and turn it into something positive you are a winner, a survivor. I was in so much pain for so long because I felt anger, sadness and betrayal. I let those things rule my life until I could accept, forgive and put the past behind me. One of the ways we did that at this seminar was by writing the names of those who had hurt us, each on a separate piece of paper. Then we ripped it up and jumped on it. Sounds crazy but it actually did work. I was able to forgive those who had caused me so much pain, but I still felt there was something missing but didn't know what. By the end of that weekend I realised the most important person I had not forgiven was myself. I didn't believe I was significant enough so I forgot about me. I still felt partly responsible for what had happened to me. I believed that I must be to blame, that I must have done something to deserve or encourage it. Once I realised I wasn't responsible because I was only a child, that they were the adults who took advantage of my youth and innocence, then I was able to forgive myself and I can never describe the feeling of utter joy I felt. I spent the next two days weeping with the joy and relief I felt was beyond words. For over fifty years, from the age of six and half, I didn't even like myself and now all of a sudden I was able to love myself. If you don't know how to love yourself, it's hard to truly love others.

I learnt then that we can let our past define us and keep us bitter as I did, or we can use it to grow and become so much more than we think we are. We can let our past glorify us and become better for it.

Fallen from Flight

... as mountains fall and crumble and as rocks
fall from a cliff ...
Job 14:18

Not long after all this happened I noticed my husband Steve withdrawing from us all. His job kept him secluded from his friends because he had to get up really early. He began to gamble quite a lot and was in quite a bit of debt. I tried to talk to him by saying we had a problem that we needed to talk about. In the past, we had always been able to talk our problems through and work them out together. But he just brushed me aside saying later, not now. But later never came.

Steve found life had become too hard, and he took his own life.

I went out one Saturday morning. We kissed, said we loved each other and said goodbye, just like we always did. But Steve wasn't there when I got home. I spent the next three days driving around and trying to find him. Having to tell my children that he was missing was one of the hardest things I have ever had to do. Eventually I went to the police to report him missing. I suggested to the police that he might have gone camping, that his fishing rod was missing. I told them to check Mitchelltown, where we went camping. They did, but couldn't find him. I felt if he had taken his fishing rod then that's where he would be, so a couple of days later I decided to go up there myself, and my eldest daughter said she would come with me. I was to meet my eldest daughter at my place, but just after I left home the detectives rang to say they wanted to see me, and were on their way to my place. I knew what they were going to say before I even answered the door to them. The Nagambie police had decided to have another look, and had found his body in his car. He had died of carbon monoxide poisoning. He had been missing for six days altogether, having taken his life the same day he got there. He set everything up, got drunk and just went to sleep. He left me a note saying he was sorry and that he loved me, which just confused me because there was no explanation. I was in shock: how could this have happened, we were supposed to be soul mates, to live our lives out together in old age, and travel around Australia. I was angry, sad, lost, totally shattered.

I hated the funeral, and practically ran out of the service as soon as it was over. I hated all the flowers at home that just kept reminding me of what I had lost, and I threw them away. My youngest daughter, her husband and their six-month-old baby stayed with me for a week, but as soon as they left I went back to work. I was doing voluntary work for my church three days a week, and I concentrated on that to help get me through.

Most of that first year without him was a blur. If I hadn't been able to talk to God, to share my pain with Him, I don't know if I would have survived. Living seemed such a bleak option. But then God reminded me my work wasn't over. I still had my family to think about. They still needed me in their lives to be a grandmother to my grandchildren and great-grandchildren. But it was so hard, every day a struggle, every day a milestone reached, every day a day of surviving. Sometimes when I was driving, I would see the truck

Steve used to drive for his work, and I would have to pull over because I would burst into tears at the memory of what I had lost. I never remarried or even had a boyfriend after that. No-one could replace Steve. He had his issues, but don't we all? It's how we deal with them that makes us different.

Steve and I had seventeen years together before he passed away. We scattered his ashes at his favourite camping spot at Major Creek where he would have wanted them. All of my children and grandchildren were there and threw a handful each.

Life does go on as they say, and I have been able to build a life on my own. I have travelled with my family, going interstate and going on a couple of cruises. I haven't been camping since Steve died. I loved it, but it was his thing. We didn't really go camping much until I met Steve, and it doesn't feel the same without him. But my family all still enjoy camping and go almost every year, so they're carrying on his tradition. They even go to his favourite place sometimes.

A couple of years after Steve died I had to stop working, due to ill health. I was a heavy smoker for fifty years and, although I quit years ago, I left it too late to save my lungs. Now I have to use oxygen to help me breathe. But I'm still active, and go out with my family, just not as much as I would like because I get out of breath very easily.

Life will always have its hardships and heartaches. That will never stop. But if we're living life with Jesus working through us, we can truly relax and let Him get us through those times. Even when I didn't believe in Him, He still believed in me. He never gave up on me as I had on Him. Having Him in our lives and handing our problems over to Him just makes those things so much easier to bear because we are not alone. God is walking with us every step of the way. I know being able to talk to God made Steve's passing easier to bear. Sometimes when I lay in bed thinking about him and having trouble falling asleep I imagine God's arms around me keeping me safe, and I know I am not alone. I feel God's presence. That always puts a smile on my face and gives me the peace I need to fall asleep.

From Sparrow to Eagle

Like an eagle that rouses her chicks and hovers over her young, so He spread His wings to take them up and carried them safely
Deuteronomy 32:11

It's how we deal with life's issues that makes or breaks us. We can succumb to the negative people in our lives and believe that what they say about us is true and blame them or ourselves for the way we are.

Or we can choose to ignore them and know that God put us all on this earth for a reason. We all have the power to rise above the negativity, the pain, the regret to become better people and use our experiences to benefit others. I have always been an optimistic person and preferred to see the good in people, to try and see the reason behind the things they do.

My purpose in life, my reasons for being here, is to be here for my family in whatever way they need me, to turn my negatives into positives, to help others believe in themselves and help them to see that they can get through anything by knowing they are not alone. I want to share with them that thousands of men and women have been through the same things. With Jesus walking with them, they too have the same power to get through anything. Yes, we can get through the hard times with our own strength, in our own way, but with Jesus beside us, in us, we have so much more inner strength and peace to help us through. Even in the worst of trauma, God has a way of taking what you can't deal with or think about until you are ready to cope with it at the right time, and then He gives it back to you when it's not so overwhelming.

You might be thinking, why bother getting to know God. After all I had managed to survive without Him in my life from the age of 26 to 54. But oh, it's so much better with Jesus walking with me and sharing the load. I have such a sense of peace and contentment that was never there before I let Jesus into my life. A sense of belonging that wasn't there before. Yes, I have my family and love them more than words can say. They are a part of me and that will never change but with Jesus it's a different kind of love. My words can't truly justify how I feel. The love, the admiration that He died on the cross for all our sins, for all eternity. The strength He gives me every day to walk my walk. For the strength He has given me just to do what I'm doing in writing my memoirs. I'm a better person with God in my life but He makes me want to be an even better person. To be as much like Christ as I possibly can be.

Finally, I am at peace with everything that has happened to me. I have been able to forgive those who have hurt me, including myself. I feel valued and worthy. I have a Father who loves me unconditionally, forever. I have nineteen beautiful grandchildren. And nine just as beautiful great-grandchildren, and, at current count, three more great-grandchildren on the way. I am content with my life, even though there are still family issues. In a large family especially, there will probably always be family issues, but that is just part of life. I am content with who I am because where I've been has made me who I have become, and I like who I have become. I believe this to be because of my walk with Jesus which has given me the extra strength I was lacking before I acknowledged Him. I am no longer a little sparrow in a yard full of cats. I am like an eagle hovering high above the earth to soar down and protect and help the other little sparrows whenever I can.